Living in Grace

An Evolving Spiritual Journey

SHARI SHEA

BALBOA.
PRESS

A DIVISION OF HAY HOUSE

Balboa Press books may be ordered through booksellers or by contacting:

Balboa Press
A Division of Hay House
1663 Liberty Drive
Bloomington, IN 47403
www.balboapress.com
1 (877) 407-4847

Because of the dynamic nature of the Internet, any web addresses or links contained in this book may have changed since publication and may no longer be valid.

The views expressed in this work are solely those of the author and do not necessarily reflect the views of the publisher, and the publisher hereby disclaims any responsibility for them.

The author of this book does not dispense medical advice or prescribe the use of any technique as a form of treatment for physical, emotional, or medical problems without the advice of a physician, either directly or indirectly. The intent of the author is only to offer information of a general nature to help you in your quest for emotional and spiritual well-being. In the event you use any of the information in this book for yourself, which is your constitutional right, the author and the publisher assume no responsibility for your actions.

Print information available on the last page.

ISBN: 978-1-5043-4489-0 (sc)
ISBN: 978-1-5043-4490-6 (e)

Balboa Press rev. date: 1/28/2016

Dedication

This book is dedicated with deepest gratitude for "My Love," Source of All, whose love and guidance mean everything to me. Knowing this Presence is the most magnificent gift of my life.

To know even one life has breathed easier because you have lived – this is to have succeeded.

– Bessie A. Stanley
(attributed to Ralph Waldo Emerson)

Contents

Foreword

When I was invited to read Shari Shea's manuscript, I approached it in full ego-mind editor mode. Is the punctuation right? Spelling? Is that sentence as clear as it should be? How can I help improve Shari's work?

Fortunately, I quickly realized that Shari's work is complete and perfect as it is. It needs no help from me. As I continued to read, I could hear Shari's voice and – what is more amazing – I could feel her Spirit.

If you are one of the many people who have experienced Shari Shea personally, you know what I mean. If you are meeting Shari here for the first time, I think you'll know her equally well as you read her book.

I know that Shari's healing power is strong and clear. I've felt its effect personally, and I've seen its effect on others. I didn't know – nor did she, I suspect – that she could channel the

Infinite from which all healing flows through the pages of a book. Now I know, and – if you allow it – you will soon know, too.

I invite you to let your ego mind focus on the words and analyze the story. That's what it does, and it does it well! At the same time, move your inner focus upward to your true Spirit self and receive *Living in Grace* at that level. Leave any judgment, comparison, or doubt with ego mind. Feel the Oneness that exists between your spirit and Shari's. Receive her story at that level.

I am especially grateful that Shari is sharing her story flat out, including muddy detours and unexpected challenges, because all our experiences are essential to the journey. After all, we aren't here to live life perfectly; we're here to live life creatively. And creativity can be messy!

The Truth is, each of us could write a book about the very same spiritual journey. The details and stories would be different for each of us, because our individual paths are unique. And yet, as infinite Beings sharing an experience of limitation, our purpose and our journey are the same. I hope this book will help you appreciate both Shari's story and your own.

I am deeply grateful to be a part of Shari's journey thus far, and I am even more grateful for her continued presence in mine. We've been through a lot together – always (well, almost always) with a shared appreciation for what is, and excitement about what will be. Whether in coffee shop chats or sacred circle ceremonies, I can always feel her healing energy. I think you will feel it, too, in these pages. I'm already eager for *Living in Grace: An Evolving Spiritual Journey – Part Two*.

And perhaps one day I'll read your story, too! The healing energy that Shari shares so beautifully can accomplish amazing things! Blessings!

Reverend Ed Townley
Ordained Unity Minister
Founder of Spirit Expressing

Acknowledgements

My husband Bob Shea, for loving me, sharing my life, and continuing to stand strong as I evolve and grow on my journey. My love for him is deep within my heart.

My children Ryan Shea and Holly Shea, for the gentle souls that they are and helping me promote my work of service. I have loved being their mother and watching them shine their lights.

My mother Sharon Alfieri, in gratitude for staying home and always taking care of me as a child.

My father Joe Alfieri, for wisdom, guidance, and sharing many spiritual adventures with me. He has been my greatest spiritual friend.

My sisters Carin Grakowsky and Sandy Linder, for being loving presences in my life.

My dear friends (you know who you are), who have supported me in my life's purpose.

Dear Lorraine Gagnon for typing this book.
Dear Bonnie Rowe for editing this book.

I love you all.

Introduction

I was guided to take pencil in hand and share with you my life thus far. This is it! I'm coming out and baring all. You will read of joys and transformations, as well as "so-called" trials and tribulations, which I moved through on my journey on this earth plane and brought me to where I am today as a Healer and Lifestyle Coach.

I trust in the truth of my experiences, that all I have moved through has been necessary for my highest growth and evolution.

Grace is a state of "being" and awareness that "I am Spirit, Divine, whole and complete"... in this present moment and always.

We are created in the image and likeness of Source, consciousness, God, energy, omnipresence. Whatever may be happening with or around us, grace affords us the ability to see things in a new light, to possibly change our perspective and paradigm. To see through the eyes of the Creator, the order and perfection in all things.

We are here to grow spiritually, as well as tap into and live our spiritual purpose. Through our work of service, we hold all brothers, sisters, and sentient beings in love and healing light. We have come from love. We are here to BE the love that we truly are.

Chapter 1

My Early Years

I was born Shari Lou Alfieri, in Houston, Texas, on March 6, 1962. When I turned one, my parents, two older sisters, and I moved to Glastonbury, Connecticut. One year later when I was two, we relocated to Marlton, New Jersey. Dad worked for the Hartford Insurance Group and transferred periodically to open and set up new offices. My mom stayed home and raised my sisters and me.

My earliest memories are from the age of two. I remember being very happy and content with my life in New Jersey. My earliest memory, in fact, is of my father changing my diaper on the bed in my upstairs bedroom. I adored the wallpaper, which was pink and white vertical striped.

I had a pet turtle that I called Myrtle, a sweet, typical name for a turtle. Myrtle lived in an oval-shaped hard rubber bucket filled with water in the corner of my bedroom. I would converse with Myrtle as if she were my friend. Eventually, she became blind and could not find her food for nourishment. She transitioned soon after that.

I can recall putting on plays in our family room with my two older sisters. Mom and Dad eagerly watched and filmed our productions. I can still hear two of the popular songs from the 1960's playing on the Hi-Fi in our living room, "Buttercup" and "Young Girl." Alongside the Hi-Fi, I remember stacks of Girl Scout cookies, as Mom was the cookie coordinator for my sister's Girl Scout troop. How I loved those Peanut Butter Patties.®

As a young child, I remember visiting Dutch Wonderland and the Hershey factory in Pennsylvania. Back then we were able to walk through the factory as they were making the chocolate.

My best friend Suzy lived two houses down from us. Her mother didn't want her to play in our sandbox because she didn't like dirt and messes. One day when Suzy was at my house playing, I talked her into a little sandbox time. Her mother saw us from her yard. Shortly thereafter, my friend was hurried home and spanked along the way. I felt bad for her and thought her mother was very mean.

This same friend and I took turns together swinging on each other's swing sets. One day while we were riding the teeter-totter on her swing set and laughing, I had a little mishap. My mother was in our backyard hanging laundry. I let go of the teeter-totter with one hand to wave to my mom. In doing so, I wobbled, hitting my head on a screw that was sticking out from a pole on the metal swing set. I began to cry and blood was streaming down my face. I can remember my mom running over, and my friend's mom running outside. My mother scooped me up, brought me inside, and laid me on my friend's kitchen table. They cleaned up my oozing wound and put some butterfly bandages on it. Lucky for me, it required no stitches. I felt very secure having my mom attend to me. And over the years, I realized how grateful I was for her being there for my sisters and me.

I have wonderful memories of the ice cream man coming down our street several times a week during the summer months. Mom always let us buy an ice cream. My favorite kind was called Chocolate Fudge Cake. It had chocolate coating on the outside, vanilla ice cream inside, and a two-inch piece of chocolate fudge in the center of the ice cream. (Interesting though, as an adult, I am not a huge fan of chocolate.) The ice cream man would sometimes throw pieces of bubble gum out of his truck onto the street for us as he drove away. What a special treat that was.

We had an above-ground pool in our backyard. One summer day when I was three or four years old, I had an unexpected underwater experience. My two older sisters were swimming with me in our pool. I wore a small inner tube for flotation. My sisters could swim and didn't need one. I watched as they freely swam around, and I wanted that same experience. I decided to take my tube off and try it out. Being unable to swim, as soon as I did this, I went straight down to the bottom of the pool. I can still remember the pristine silence and overwhelming peace I felt. Everything was so still and calm. It wasn't long though, before my mom, who was a few feet away conversing with a neighbor, took notice of a few strands of my hair at the surface of the pool water. She lunged over the rail of the pool and pulled me up. I remember coughing and choking a bit, but all was well.

Once in a while, Dad would bring my sisters and me to his office in Philadelphia on a Saturday morning. Oh, how I marveled at the typewriter, pretending to be a secretary. Dad let us get a candy bar from the machine; this felt like a Christmas present.

When I was four years old, I was to attend nursery school. I remember my mom sitting me on the kitchen counter and talking to me about school. I reached for a jar that had some peanut brittle in it and broke off a piece. As I enjoyed the treat, I remember saying to my mom, "I don't want to leave you all alone, Mommy." Mom said, "Don't worry honey, I'll be fine and you will have a lot of fun at nursery school." When the first day of school came, I kept hugging my mom, not wanting to let her go as we walked down the hallway. (I had similar experiences with my own daughter when she entered school.) Nursery school turned out to be quite fun for me. I loved listening to stories, painting, coloring, and snack time. I can still taste the watered-down grape juice and vanilla wafers.

My kindergarten year was not a fond memory for me. My teacher was very old and very grouchy. We were bused to a church for our class. My teacher complained to my mom that I chewed on my pearl necklace, which Mom had given me, during class. My mom told my teacher that she didn't have a problem with that. That pearl is now entwined on a dream catcher that hangs in my sanctuary.

One day at kindergarten, I ate a raisin from the basket before it was snack time. My teacher saw me, grabbed my ear, and walked me to a time-out chair outside the classroom. I have always wavered at following rules. Mom shared with me years later that my teacher's husband was very ill and she had to work. This helped me understand why she had always seemed so angry.

First grade flowed a bit better for me. My teacher was understanding of my lack of focus and concentration on my schoolwork. I struggled with the academic process, and this was challenging for me throughout my school years.

As the years have gone on, I have come to embrace the fact that although I struggled with academics in school, I have excelled in "Human

Relations." As I am continuously growing in my spiritual journey, I have had the honor and privilege to help and coach many folks with their journey.

Chapter 2

The Move that Rocked My World

When I was seven years old, Dad accepted a job transfer to Hartford, Connecticut. It was early in the second grade for me when we were to make the move. My teacher in New Jersey had invited our entire class to her wedding, which was to take place in the spring. I would not be able to attend. I felt sad for this and for leaving my very best friend Suzy. My sisters had the okay from Mom not to attend their last day of school before the move. I decided to stay home as well. A classmate who lived down the street came by after school to say goodbye to me. He told me that a party had been planned for me that day. I felt sad in knowing that I had missed it.

On moving day in October 1969, as our car pulled out of the driveway for the last time, my family all cried except for my father. One of my sister's best friends rode his bike alongside our car as long as he could. He lost his balance and fell off his bike while crying. I am reliving the feelings I had on this day, as it was a turning point in my childhood. Those of you who know me well may find it hard to believe, but I was a shy, quiet, and insecure child. I was leaving behind my familiar world.

We moved to Poquonock, which is a part of Windsor, Connecticut, and named after the Poquonock Indians. I began second grade at Poquonock Elementary School in late October. I felt like an outsider from the start. Most of the other children had already established friendships and groups from the first two months of the school year. I also was not confident enough to really put myself out there and make friends. One girl and a boy included me in their play at recess. We would run around outside playing a game called "Witchy Poo." One person was the witch, who tried to capture the other two. This helped me integrate a bit, but I still yearned for New Jersey. I felt lost and despondent. I remember asking my father several times, "Daddy, when are we going to move back to our other house?"

My hair was a reddish color. A couple of boys used to tease me and poke me. This made me very sad. When I spoke to my mom about this, she said, "Oh, Shari, just ignore them." Later, when I was eighteen years old, one of the boys asked me out. I turned him down, remembering how tormented I felt by his behavior toward me many years before. I have since forgiven him and realize he was probably just flirting with me.

Through the next four school years, until I reached the seventh grade, I wondered if I would ever be happy again. During these years, my saving grace seemed to be summertime. We had a built-in pool at the side of our yard. My next door neighbor was a year younger than I. I took on a bit of a bossy demeanor toward her, as she was even more timid than I. We did, however, have lots of fun together. After a good swim, we would place our towels on the hot paved driveway and lie on our tummies to warm up from the water. We took turns bringing out a snack from each other's house to share. I'll never forget the Carr's whole wheat crackers with cream cheese on top that my friend shared with me. Yummy! Sometimes we tent-camped in the side of my yard. I will always remember the smell of the vinyl cloth tent from childhood. My friend and I played school many times. Being the bossy one, I usually wound up being the teacher.

I have great memories of summer evenings after dinner playing "4-Square" with my sister Sandy, another friend from across the street, and some older girls from another street. The older girls were very nice to me. My sister Sandy and I became closer after our move to Connecticut and throughout the rest of our childhood. She did, however, keep very busy, as she studied and worked very hard at her grades. She always made honors and high honors. We were so opposite in this way.

I enjoyed playing the clarinet from fourth to eleventh grade.

During the 1970's my favorite TV shows were The Waltons, Little House on the Prairie, and the Brady Bunch.

My family and I attended a Catholic Mass held at 11:30 a.m. every Sunday. This was at Mom's insistence. We sat in the second pew every week. I felt comforted by a beautiful statue of Mary in front of my seat. Our church was right across the street from the elementary school I attended. This made things very convenient for catechism, one day a week after school.

The first several years, the nuns taught us. I made my First Communion, but felt like I hadn't really learned anything. I hated confession, and I disliked our priest, who I felt was loud and mean. By the time I was eleven or twelve, catechism was held in the lower level of the church. We were taught by parents who volunteered their time.

These years of teaching were based around the life of Jesus, my earliest and fondest learnings of this holy man. His teachings were of love and kindness, along with forgiveness: his compassion for all of humanity, his yearning for everyone to be whole, and his lack of judgment of a brother or sister, no matter what their beliefs.

In his lifetime, I believe Jesus helped all who yearned for healing to connect with their faith and higher self to bring about their desired outcome. Even though we were warned by our priest to beware of God's wrath, I didn't believe him. I always felt a peacefulness and caring when I thought of God's Presence, which felt like a comfy father figure.

I am grateful that we can choose what we want to believe in life and about life. Joel

Osteen says, "We can be bitter, or we can be better" and "We can be victims, or we can be victors." We can move ahead fearlessly in the face of all seeming adversity. I have chosen to be victorious.

Chapter 3

Middle School Vulnerability

I was happy for a fresh start at seventh grade Junior High. I was now attending school with kids from several other elementary schools in Windsor. I was feeling more confident about making some new friends. My insecurities, however, led me to be a follower, smoking my first cigarette at age twelve and having my first beer at age thirteen. These years are so significant for girls and boys, who are experiencing hormonal changes and the onset of puberty.

One of the things which helped me remain somewhat "grounded" was the beginning of a more meaningful friendship with two girls who lived on my street. We frequently would get together and have singing contests. We would vote on a grade of one, two, or three, with one being the highest grade. "Killing Me Softly with

His Song" was one of our regular songs. We sang without any music. I usually did the best, being voted number one almost every time. This greatly helped my self-esteem, as my grades in school were nothing to write home about.

I met another girl who had just moved into our neighborhood when we were eleven years old. She and I played "closet Barbies" until we were thirteen. You see, it wasn't cool to play Barbies if you were in middle school.

I have fond memories through these years of visiting both sets of grandparents in upper state New York. I can still remember the smell of Ivory soap from our bath at Gram and Grampa Lynd's house. And I remember playing house, pretending to be an adult, at Grandma and Grandpa Alfieri's home. I so wanted to grow up!

One day, a boy at school asked me if I wanted to "bang." I didn't answer him. To be honest, I didn't know what that meant until later when I asked a friend. It meant "Do you want to have sex?" We were twelve years old at the time. Boy, did I have a lot to learn!

Our school had a yearly ski trip. I wasn't on the ski team, so I was not part of the trip. A few of the twelve-year-old boys decided to get drunk the night before. They had to have their stomachs pumped and missed out on the trip. I remember feeling so sorry for them.

These years were a time of many boyfriend/girlfriend relationships. I had my first kiss and boyfriend when I was twelve. We met square dancing. He was a really nice boy, but I began to like another square dancer, so he and I broke up. By the time I was fourteen, I was smoking cigarettes on and off and drinking with friends once in a while. My boyfriend at the time was wild and free-spirited like me. I am grateful though, that I respected myself and my body. I was not going to be used and tossed aside. Having sex seemed to be the general M.O. for many kids my age, but not for me. Alas, because I would not give of myself this way, my boyfriend broke up with me after a few months. I was devastated, as I really liked him, but life went on.

Many times throughout these years of schooling, I would lose the "present" moment in conversations with friends. It felt like I left and then came back, feeling totally lost in what they were talking about. I could not understand this phenomenon at the time. I now realize I had left my body and then returned.

Chapter 4

The Wild Child

When I attended high school, it was from the tenth to twelfth grade. I had some major wild oats to sow! I was footloose and fancy-free. When there was a party, I was there – indoor at someone's home, or outdoor with a bonfire, even better. I loved the excitement of not knowing if we would get caught and chased away. I partied pretty heavily and had many nights when I know my "angels brought me home." I am so grateful for all of the "guiding ones" who watched over me as I moved through the experiences that were mine to live out at that time. I dated several boys in high school. The relationships broke up either because I was a "no" girl or because I simply lost interest in them.

I had a couple of car accidents in high school. My car hit and bent a telephone pole. I was a junior in high school, very much "under the influence," driving from one graduation party to another. In the other accident I knocked down a light pole with my bumper. I drove off, and someone wrote down my license plate. I had to go to court before a judge. He asked me why I left the scene. I said, "I was scared and didn't know what to do," which was basically the truth. The judge let me off without punishment. Thankfully, those were my only accidents involving my car in high school.

It was commonplace to smoke cigarettes in the girls' bathroom, and we never got caught. I was smoking full time by high school. We were actually allowed to smoke cigarettes in the outdoor courtyard during our lunch break.

I experienced many rock concerts. The creepiest one was The Grateful Dead.

I had fun at both of my proms, as well as at other dances. I never did, however, become involved in any school activities. This certainly would have helped give me a more balanced direction. I had many friends in high school, and I truly began to feel as though I belonged. They were crazy years, but fun as well. I have no regrets. It was a miracle that I graduated from high school and kept my virginity as well.

Please note. I was guided to be up front and honest with those of you reading this book. It is my hope that in some way what I have shared thus far will help some of you to accept and love yourself even though there were times you may have lived less than spiritually-focused lives.

The fall after high school graduation, I began attending a local community college. I also had finally met and began dating the older brother of one of my best friends from high school. Let's just say in hindsight, he was not the best influence on me. I was, however, able to hold down my twenty-hour a week job at a day care center. (I loved being around children and still do to this day.)

I did really well at the community college. I really enjoyed the Early Childhood Education Program and graduated with an Associate's degree two years later.

Still with the same boyfriend, after experiencing many highs and lows in our relationship, I was beginning to wonder if this person was in my best interest. You see, we partied a lot, smoked a lot, and listened only to heavy rock music. We had some wild and crazy times. My boyfriend was very negative about life and didn't feel he wanted to bring children into this world. I, on the other hand, loved life, loved kids, and wanted to someday get married and have children. I decided it would be best if we took a break from our relationship. We broke up for one month. After this, he persuaded me to get back together with him. I agreed and we were together for one more year.

I enrolled in a four-year state college and attended college for one more school year. During this year, I began to change. I began listening to cassette tapes of John Denver's music. I had always loved being and playing outside as a child. His music reignited my soul's stirring for greater joy and enjoyment in life. My boyfriend was not pleased with my music selection. I also quit fulltime smoking and heavy drinking. I had only a few cigarette on the weekends with a small amount of social drinking. I was changing. I was "cleaning up my act," as they say. After my third year of college, I decided to quit school. I wanted to find a fulltime job and make more money for a while. Finishing school at some point was a possibility, but I wasn't sure. I also ended my three-year relationship with my boyfriend. It was time for a fresh start.

Chapter 5

Time to Grow Up

It was June of 1983. I was young and enthusiastic, with vim and vigor. I was single but having fun dating a few guys. My father worked for the Hartford Insurance Group. He landed me an interview at a local branch of The Hartford. My interview panned out, and I was hired in August. My title was Loss Cash Processor. My job primarily was to thumb through stacks of papers to find those requested by Underwriters, and Billing and Claims personnel via the computer. I sorted them by code numbers. Then I delivered the papers requested to each person in our building. The nice part about this was that I would occasionally meet new people and I had the ability to move around. I bought myself some business clothes, which I enjoyed wearing.

That December, four months into my new employment, the branch office held a Christmas party at a local venue. I went to the party with some new girlfriends from work. Early on in the night, I was asked to dance by a young man. I agreed and we danced most of the night together. I would never have believed this at the time, but nine months later Bob and I were married. Bob really helped me grow up. He was more mature and grounded than I was.

We connected on a deep level very quickly in our relationship. He was so kind and giving. He was full of life, energy, and enthusiasm. He accepted and marveled at my free-spirited nature. We were very much in love. He was very mature and level-headed. We shared similar values. Although I thought I would spend some time in travel and other pursuits before settling down, I know we had been brought together to marry and raise a family. Only three short months into our relationship, he proposed and I said yes. We wed six months later on September 15, 1984. Bob and I had some arguments in that first year of marriage. Truly we were deeply in love but still had so much to learn about one another.

We bought our first home the following spring, in 1985. I left my clerical job at The Hartford and took a nanny position with a family with three children. I loved my work and have always been so comfortable around children.

One year later, in June of 1986, I became pregnant. We were both surprised, as we expected to wait a bit longer, but we looked forward to being parents. Unfortunately, at the start of my sixth month, now twenty-four weeks pregnant, our baby transitioned while in the womb. I was twenty-four and Bob was twenty-seven. We were told that it was a spontaneous stillbirth. I was induced into labor at the hospital and had to deliver the fetus. I truly felt like I was in shock and disbelief. Bob and I moved through this experience together. We received news from my doctor that it was not a genetic defect in the fetus, and we could have healthy children moving forward. I went back to work the next week. Caring for the three small children that I adored kept me from over-thinking what had happened.

Four months later, I was pregnant again. I had a wonderful pregnancy. I gave birth to Ryan, our son, in January of 1988. This was such a joyful and amazing time. I quit my nanny job and began the job that I really looked forward to the most, raising my own family. Ryan was a fussy baby with colic, but I enjoyed him tremendously! Three years later, his sister Holly joined our family and my life felt complete.

Bob had taken a new job when Ryan was a baby. He worked longer hours, but we made it all work. By the time the kids were ages five and two, Bob branched off from the parent company he had been working for and began to run his own show. Travel was required and it was not always easy. Family dinners, games, and holiday adventures were a priority for us. We had several fun trips to Disney World over the years. Bob and I made time for "us" as a couple and kept our marriage strong. We have always had great, open communication in our relationship. This has been a great factor in our long-term marriage.

As the years rolled by, I became involved with activities at the kids' school. I felt very fulfilled and happy to see them during school hours. I was a room mom, helped in their classrooms, went with them on school field trips, and helped out in the school library and school store. I was also Holly's Girl Scout leader for a few years. Bob was Ryan's pack leader for a couple of years. He helped out with Ryan's den and camped with the Scouts as well. Ryan patterned after his dad and became an Eagle Scout. That was a very proud moment for us! I was a carpool mom for Holly's gymnastics group for several years. We enjoyed so many performances and shows that she was involved in. Proud moments!

I have many fond memories of family camping with Bob and the kids. We did so a couple of times each summer for many years. This afforded us great quality time together. We all pitched in, putting up the tent, gathering firewood, readying for meals, cleaning up, etc. Let's not forget toasting marshmallows, bike rides, family games, and swimming in the lake.

We also spent a lot of time at home with our kids. We took hikes, bike rides, and had picnic lunches. We enjoyed many nights of Hide and Go Seek after dinner. We played board games and cards.

Chapter 6

From Challenge to Triumph and New Awakenings

When Ryan and Holly were ages eight and five, I became a vegetarian. I was a vegan for the first two years, but found it to be too restrictive after a while. The year after turning vegetarian, I was faced with a serious health challenge. I was experiencing a series of abnormal pap smears at the gynecologist. After the New Year, in January of 1998, a biopsy revealed that I had a severe pre-cancerous condition. It was level three cervical dysplasia.

I was literally scared to death by this diagnosis. At my doctor's request, I was to have cryosurgery in three weeks. I can remember my teeth chattering as I revealed the news to Bob over the phone. That evening, after the kids went to bed, I had a good cry on the floor in our study. I did not have a strong prayer life at this point in my life. My family and I, however, had been attending a very nice progressive Congregational Church for about three years. We wanted our children to be instilled with faith and an awareness of a Higher Power. I did believe in a master plan, that is, a God of some sort.

During my crying spell on the study floor, I can recall saying, "So this is it, God? I am going to die and my kids are going to grow up without their mother?" As I lay there, these words came to me: "No, you're not going to die. In the morning, call your friend Chris and ask for Reiki treatments." Chris had just recently become Reiki certified. After I shared my challenge with her, she agreed to offer me Reiki treatments three times a week for three weeks. She would not take any money from me. I tithed to her with purchases of aroma oils, natural soaps, and trinkets.

I was guided by my friend and naturopathic doctor to juice three times a day. Carrot juice has been known to heal and ward off cancer. I boosted up my Superfood Plus (a blue-green algae, vitamin, and mineral drink), which

I purchased from Dr. Richard Schultze's American Botanical Pharmacy. I ate more garlic.

I began connecting with God every night, asking for continual guidance. I was guided toward forgiveness of myself and others who I perceived had hurt me. My father gave me Neale Donald Walsch's *Conversations with God: An Uncommon Dialogue (Book 1)*. I practiced the "I AM" principles daily. After my walk each day, I would stand in my yard, admiring the trees, proclaiming, "I AM one with you. I love you." I began reciting "I Am Perfect Health" with feeling in my heart, as well as trust and faith. Dad had given me his "reality prayer," which reveals loving truths for oneself.

I began to simplify my life to a greater degree. It felt good to give away things, even things of value that I no longer needed or wanted. I had a tag sale and de-cluttered many of my possessions, as they were possessing me. I felt so light and free.

My dear friend, who had offered me healing for three weeks, was approaching her moving day to South Carolina. At our last session together, I had a deep sense that I no longer needed the surgery. I called my doctor to see if she would do another biopsy. She said she was standing by her results. She suggested I get a second opinion, but not to wait too long. You see, I was only one level before the onset of cancer. I had to listen to my heart and take the risk.

My naturopathic doctor friend recommended someone to me. I had all of my records transferred to this female gynecologist. She asked me to tell her what I had been doing to help myself. I shared my story with her. She biopsied me that day. When the results came back, they showed that my condition had regressed two levels during that three-week holistic healing period. This brought me to level one dysplasia. At this level they keep a watch on it for a few months to see if it progresses further. When I went back three months later, it was completely gone. I am grateful to say that I never had the surgery. Through the combination of my faith in "Our Beloved" and my own spirit, I was healed.

This experience was one of the greatest blessings of my life. It prompted me to think of giving back in service what had been given to me. I felt very drawn to train in Reiki healing. I became a certified Reiki practitioner in 1999. I know that my experience with "dis-ease" was needed to help heal some unresolved hurts and also to move me forward with healing service to humanity. My gynecologist, and now dear friend, began referring some of her patients to me for lifestyle coaching and energy healing. One person came weekly for two years. Others came here and there. I was overjoyed to be serving in this way.

That summer of 1999 my dad, who had been working with the Kriya Yoga Breath technique, came across an advertisement from the Ananda Village, a spiritual community in California. A couple from this village had recently opened a branch in Rhode Island called Ananda East. With great yearning in my soul to connect more deeply with Creator, I suggested to my dad that we attend the Summer Weekend Outdoor Retreat. We did. We slept in a large Boy Scout tent with cots. Being a camper, I was right at home. The shower was enclosed, but outside. This was very exhilarating! We attended different sessions during the day. They offered meditation, yoga class, and other activities as well.

The activity that really stands out in my mind was a nature walk through the woods, one of my favorite things in life to do. The walk was led by Joseph Cornell, who had written a beautiful book entitled *With Beauty Before Me*. He lives and works at Ananda Village in California and travels as he teaches people how to connect with nature. As I mentioned, he led us on a meditative journey through the wooded property of the Center. Once we entered a deep area in the woods, we were told to find a tree and sit or lie down under it. As I lay down under my chosen tree, an overwhelming sense of calm and serenity came over me. As I think back on this moment in time, I can honestly say that I experienced one the most blissful moments of my life. I felt pure joy and ecstasy as I lay beneath the leafed canopy with my Beloved. We were each asked to describe our feelings during this ten-minute period of peace. When it was my turn, I became so choked up with tear-filled emotion that it was difficult to speak. I am hopeful that all of you reading this will have at least one experience like this in your life that you can treasure.

The very next year in May 2000, Ananda East was blessed with a visit from Swami Kriyananda. This amazing being was a direct disciple of Paramhansa Yogananda. Dad and I were excited to be in attendance. It was a cold and rainy day. The event was held outside in a tent in order to accommodate the group of people gathered. Swami spoke of peace, living in harmony with one another, and forgiveness. He had some funny stories of mishaps between different spiritually-minded people. He even poked fun at Yogananda. The second after he did so, Yogananda's large picture, which had been on the table behind him, blew over face down. We all laughed, and Swami said, "Oh, I guess I'd better watch myself." Everyone shared lunch afterward in the couple's home right next to the tent. It was so wonderful to meet this amazing guru and literally feel his peace and contentment.

Swami made a repeat appearance to Ananda East one year later. Dad and I attended once again. This year, the day was beautiful and sunny. Each time I attended, being in Swami's presence, I felt somehow transformed. It would be another two years until Dad and I had our next spiritual adventure "away."

In 2003 Dad and I attended a small intimate spiritual retreat in Saugerties, New York. The hosts were John and Jan Price. John, known in the world of publication as John Randolph Price, is the founder of Quartus, a monthly spiritually-inspirational newsletter. He is also the author of several books, including *The Superbeings* and *The Jesus Code*. Both John and Jan's love, compassion, and kindness were felt by all thirty participants. I truly began to connect with Spirit at a deeper level over the weekend.

Jan shared with us of her near death experience (NDE). She didn't want to come back to this earth plane after experiencing joyful flow and contentment on the other side. John taught the importance of relaxing and enjoying life. He stressed "being" more than "doing." He spoke of allowing the Universe to flow through and all around us, offering balance and harmony in all of our endeavors.

I headed home after that weekend feeling empowered and more deeply connected with Source. Sadly, this wonderful new stimulation lasted for only a month.

During this time, I had begun a part-time caregiving position for a baby girl. Being a "mommy" again to a little one brought me great joy. My daughter Holly was very happy as well, almost as if she had a baby sister she could help take care of. Two and a half years later the child I cared for welcomed a baby sister. We have had a lot of fun over the past twelve years. The sisters call me their second mother.

Chapter 7

Born Again in Spirit

As the feeling of separation from Source rolled back in, I began to feel extremely restless. I told my husband that I needed to get away alone for a couple of days. I checked into an inn two towns over from my home. I went for strolls around the quaint little town. I sat in the silence in my room and asked for help. "Show me the way," I remember saying to Spirit. "I don't know how to find you at that beautiful, deeper level again." No answer came to me that weekend, but soon after, a situation came about that would change me forever.

My father had heard of a man by the name of Ron Roth through the Hay House organization. He ordered a set of four audio cassettes by Ron, listened to them, and put them aside. About a week later, he listened to them again; then he gave them to me. I listened to one tape. As Ron was speaking, "First comes the thought, then comes the spoken word (feeling you already have your desire), then you give it to the Universe to do its thing." The next thing I heard was Ron banging his fist on a table, and he proclaimed in a loud voice, "The process will never change!" Well I just about fell off my chair in delight! This was it, I just knew it! This was the teacher I had been waiting for!

I called my dad right away and said, "When is Ron Roth speaking and where?" This was the fall of 2003. Dad and I made plans to attend the next four-day retreat with Ron Roth and Celebrating Life Ministries (CLM) in April 2004. Just knowing I would be part of this retreat eased my mind. My restlessness subsided. Other issues were at hand. My husband was becoming a little nervous that I had other interests outside of our family. I assured him that some spiritual time for me was equal to his time playing golf. Thankfully, this made sense to him. You see, other than the one weekend I spent with my father while attending the Ananda East retreat, and one weekend in Saugerties, New York, Bob had not been left alone with our children.

I experienced so many changes within my being at the April 2004 CLM retreat. Dad and I flew into Chicago, arriving the morning of the retreat. We arrived at the Hyatt Hotel in Oakbrook, Illinois, at 9 a.m., as it was starting. We left our bags in the back of the room and found seats as close as we could to the front. We were in the right side section around seven rows back. When Ron Roth walked in the room and around our side up to the platform, my heart leapt with joy in anticipation.

After greeting everyone, Ron took us through a meditation/healing process. We pictured ourselves walking into a brightly lit cave. As we approached a big rock, Jesus was sitting there. Jesus opened his arms, drawing us near. He invited us to sit on his lap. He embraced us with the most warm and encompassing hug one had ever felt. He told us that we were so loved, and very safe. After this, Ron invited us to reflect and then invite departed loved ones or friends who had crossed over. Were we still missing them or saddened that we hadn't a chance to say goodbye? I thought of my paternal grandparents who transitioned just one month apart from each other when my daughter was only seven months old. My dad's parents were living in a little town called Warsaw, about an hour south of Buffalo, New York. I didn't want to take my infant daughter on that long car ride and upset her routine and schedule. I therefore declined to attend either funeral. As a result, I never felt complete with their transitions. The experience that Ron was helping us through allowed me to speak to and embrace my grandparents. I told them that I loved and missed them. I asked for understanding about why I hadn't been able to be at their services. This experience offered me release and closure.

On day number two, during the afternoon session, something astonishing happened to me. Everyone was sitting down when the music began playing a song of praise and worship. Ron walked to the platform. He asked us to stand while singing. Dad stood right up and so did everyone around me. I tried to, but I couldn't move my body. I only had movement of my head and neck. I turned to Dad and said, "I can't get up." He shared his "Italian sarcasm" and said, "Then don't. Just sit there." He had no idea that I literally could not get up. I felt a small amount of fear, but more bewilderment than anything else. As I sang the song, tears streamed constantly down my face. After a period of about ten minutes, I was able to move again. I felt light and overjoyed. Later that day after talking with a couple of participants, they shared this phrase with me called "frozen in the Spirit." They told me that I was most likely experiencing some intense emotional healing. I felt so amazingly grateful.

On the third morning of the retreat, I sat "present" as Ron spoke of love, generosity, and kindness. Suddenly I began feeling intense heat over my upper and lower chest area. I then felt heat behind my right thigh and up to my buttocks. I had been experiencing a lot of heartburn for a few months, along with sciatic nerve pain on the right for about a year. The feeling of intense heat lasted only a few minutes. When the sensation subsided, I felt an amazing sense of calm and peace within me. I began sobbing, feeling overwhelmed with gratitude. Since that day, the pain in both those areas has never returned.

During a retreat, a healing service was usually offered a few times. One such service was held on Sunday. It was Ron's Interfaith Communion Service, which I had never experienced before. Everyone lined up in a long line. The ushers organized how many could stand in the line at one time. There were catchers who moved behind people, as Ron walked along and touched some, and offered words to others. Many people fell backward to the floor. It is called "being slain" or "resting in the Spirit."

I had previously witnessed that at a Miracle Service that my father brought our family to in Rhode Island when I was thirteen. Kathryn Kulhman was the spiritual healing Evangelist who facilitated the service. For many years now, I have aspired to be like Kathryn. I admired the driving commitment and devotion for "Our Beloved" by which she lived her life.

Relating back to Ron's intensive healing service, I did not "rest in the Spirit." My heart, however, did palpitate quite a bit when Ron walked before me. Now it was my turn before Ron. He gently placed his finger on my throat chakra area. I didn't realize it then, as I do now, that I was being cleansed so that I would move forward in speaking my Truth in order to offer the healing work I was being called to do.

The musicians and their music were otherworldly. I felt strongly connected with Spirit and was feeling love for everyone else as well. Dad and I made several new friends at that retreat, many of whom we still connect with and some we still see to this day, ten years later.

When the retreat was over, we waited in line to thank Ron. I told him that I had never cried so much during a period of four days before. Ron said to me, "...mostly tears of Joy. Now go and share."

I had already purchased Ron's first book, *The Healing Path of Prayer.* I eagerly awaited reading it on the airplane. As Dad and I left the retreat and rode to the airport, I found myself among non-retreat-goers for the first time in four days and felt a bit of aftershock for all I had experienced. Since we arrived at the airport with only carry-on luggage, we proceeded to the security line. I looked at the people all around me and felt the most unbelievable sense of love and compassion for each one of them. I wanted to shout out "I love you, I love all of you!" I had always felt myself to be very accepting and understanding of others. This was different. It was a new perception that I was literally "one with all people." This feeling was of an unconditional love that I had never felt before. I marveled in its delicious flavor.

I read almost all of Ron's book on the flight home. I also felt a greater ease and safety with flying that had escaped me since 9/11. After returning home, I began meditating every morning regularly.

Dad and I began a volunteer job together called Meals on Wheels. We deliver prepared meals to elderly or disabled folks in my town. The meals cost a very nominal fee. Dad and I have made some amazing friendships with many wonderful people. Our true inspirations are friends in their 90's, still sharp as a tack. They have shared with us their wit, humor, and amazing life experiences.

Chapter 8

Healing and Prophecy

It was now the summer of 2004. My son Ryan taught me how to email. Boy, did he have his hands full with me! "Duh" doesn't even come close. Patient he was and still is! My daughter has been my saving grace as well. I have made her my assistant, helping to type flyers for my services. My children are two of the greatest blessings in my life.

After a month or two, my meditations were lasting one hour each morning. I was so amazed that during the five months between the first and second Celebrating Life Ministries (CLM) intensives (April to September) I was fostering a magnificent relationship with my Beloved. This continued to grow and flourish. I stayed feeling empowered and confident in myself and my evolving unfoldment in my spiritual journey.

The Healing Path of Prayer proved to be a great tool in teaching me how to meditate and contemplate. Ron reminded us that we all have the opportunity to actually "know God" and not just know "of or about God." In his book, Ron recommended a method of taking in three deep breaths, slowly and steadily, concentrating on the breath to help ease us to a calm state for meditation. He advised using the invocation in his book (or making up one of our own), and stressed the importance of love and devotion for "Creator," as well as understanding that "Spirit is everywhere and in all things." This is referred to as Omnipresence. Whenever I stop and think of my Beloved's Presence, I become awestruck – when the wind blows in my hair, when the sun warms my face, or when I feel the breath of nature. Every breath is Spirit breathing through me, through all of us. He taught that spirituality was actually simple; however, living this principle is not always easy. It requires discipline, commitment, perseverance, dedication, and devotion. Family and friends may not like or support what we are doing. How strong can we be in standing up for what we know to be our Truth, our calling, and purpose?

Ron was not a big fan of having lots of rules to follow, nor the need for specific techniques, thankfully. Given my history, nor was I. "If you adopt a technique and it works for you, great!...but don't marry a method!" he would warn. I loved that statement, for if we do marry a method, we will then close ourselves off for growth and change in that area. How can we be open to all sorts of possibilities, if we feel there is only one way to do, be, or act on any given thing? Charles Fillmore, co-founder of Unity, said, "I reserve the right to change my mind." Whoo hoo! Go, Charlie!

I later went to the CLM website and learned that Ron would be leading a group of people to Brazil. They would be traveling to the Casa de Dom Inácio (the house of St. Ignatius Loyola) in Abadiânia, Brazil, where a healer/spiritual medium worked by the name of João de Deus (John of God). I so wanted to go. First, I let my husband know that I wanted to attend the fall CLM retreat in Illinois. He wasn't too happy about that, saying, "Will you be wanting to go on two retreats a year now?" I said that I didn't know yet, but that I also wanted to go to Brazil the following May 2005, as Ron was leading a group to a very sacred place. Well, poor Bob had to sit down for that one. I will say that we were able to talk everything through. Bob even transferred his airline miles to Dad and me so we could fly business class to Brazil, making our long journey much more relaxing. It was so kind of him. More on that later.

Since I was meditating every morning, I was feeling so much more connected to Creator for much of the time. I felt more tuned in with my healing work and was eager for more. During that summer, however, a growth had manifested on my right upper eyelid. I went to a general practitioner to have it checked. She said it was not a tumor, but rather some type of solid mass and I would have to see a plastic surgeon for its removal. It was growing at a slow pace. I had decided to wait until after the retreat to follow through with its removal.

The second CLM retreat was as powerful as the first, but in different ways. Dad and I had already established friendships with many from the first retreat, so it was great to see everyone again. We all immediately clicked and felt like a family. Dad and I had both joined the Educational Program. This entitled us to come a day early for what they called "Family Day." There, we encountered about twenty-five people who had been through the Educational Program as ordained ministers or through the Spirit of Peace Monastic Community as professed monks. Having been founded by Ron, the latter community was conducted by invitation only from Ron himself, after learning of someone's service to the world for humanity's sake. The former included students of the Educational Program, of which my father and I were now a part. Since the size of the group was no more than twenty-five in number, we felt as though we were experiencing a personal teaching from Ron, making it feel very special for us.

I moved with the flow of the retreat as it was unfolding, right from the beginning. I felt so "at one" with Divine Presence. There was joy overflowing within my being every minute of every day. Two days before the retreat ended, there was a healing service in the afternoon. As Ron walked down the center aisle, I felt elated with ecstasy. He walked past me and then paused. Reaching out to me, he held his hand in mine for about five seconds. He looked into my eyes and nodded his head.

Previous to this, I had been wondering whether healing was my true calling. I had been seeing some clients but not with regular flow, except for one person who saw me weekly. Now, thanks to Ron, a prophecy was revealed to me. In those brief seconds of eye transmission, I heard "You will do this work as I am doing." In honesty, I understood what was said, but I wasn't sure how the process would unfold. My husband's boat was already being rocked with my wanting to attend an Intensive plus a pilgrimage in the same year. Besides, I was a stay-at-home mom with two children, age thirteen and sixteen. Surely, this was not going to flow with him. This prophecy brought great excitement and also some fear and anxiety. Questions and tensions mounted, and I could barely eat for the remaining two days.

Clarity on that was to come in the second part of the service. We were to line up, walk around the room and each have a chance to stand before Ron for a message. As I proceeded in the line, my body began to tremble – not so surprising, given the previous prophecy. My heart was beating very rapidly. I remember reciting one of Ron's calming affirmations, "Peace to my thoughts, peace to my feelings, peace to my emotions, peace to my body." Thankfully, I was able to calm myself down. Before I knew it, it was my turn. He said, "Okay, you don't have to wonder anymore. You know the path to take. Now go into meditation and the wisdom will come to you." Well, I just about fainted right then and there. After the telepathic transmission I had just received twenty minutes earlier came the verbal confirmation of it! I was excited and overwhelmed at the same time. Later, it would finally dawn on me that when a prophecy is revealed in part or whole, it does not mean that it is about to unfold at that very moment. I spent the last two days of the retreat trying to process all that I had experienced.

The morning after arriving home, I noticed something that astonished me. The growth on my eyelid was gone. It had not shrunk. Rather, it was completely gone! To this day, it has never reappeared. I was and still am so grateful for yet another amazing blessing!

In the eight months that followed, I meditated every morning and evening as well. I could feel transformations occurring. Were the "entities" of the healer, John of God, preparing me for the pilgrimage to Brazil? Dad and I prepared ourselves for what was to be an amazing transformation.

Chapter 9

My Sacred Pilgrimage to Abadiânia, Brazil

May 15, 2005, the day had finally arrived for Dad and me to join Ron Roth, Paul Funfsinn (Ron's associate, later President of CLM), and a group of one hundred or more people for a most sacred pilgrimage to Brazil. We would be in Brazil for two weeks. Words can never do justice in describing how blessed we felt for this opportunity! It was a very long journey, but we arrived safely. We had a full day to relax outside at our pousada (guesthouse). The next day was Tuesday, the day before three days of Casa visits (Casa de Dom Inácio – house of St. Ignatius Loyola) with João de Deus (John of God). On Wednesday, Thursday, and Friday of each week, João works at the Casa. If you are not familiar with John of God, you can read about his life of healing and mediumship online.

Again, it was now Tuesday, the day before our Casa day with João. We had the opportunity to walk down to the Casa early in the morning. It was very quiet there. Only the volunteers like Dad and me, and the regular kitchen workers were there. We were able to help in cutting vegetables for the blessed soups that would be prepared later that day.

João blesses the soup each week after it is made. All who come to the Casa on one or all three days of the working week receive a bowl of blessed soup after the morning "Current Session." Briefly, "current" refers to energy. Those who "sit in Current" in prayer and meditation help hold the energy and vibration collectively to a level that enhances the work of the "entities," who offer healing assistance to those who visit the Casa. The entities are discarnate beings from other dimensions. Many of them have lived lives before as prominent doctors, scholars, and so on.

It felt like a great honor for Dad and me, knowing we had a hand literally in helping prepare the soup.

I awoke very early Wednesday morning, eager for the first day at the Casa. The food was absolutely amazing and much of it was vegetarian, which was perfect for me. We walked in a group down the long street to the Casa grounds with our beautiful Casa guides from California, Diana Rose and Bob Dinga. Diana and Bob guide groups at the Casa five times per year. That is the maximum amount of time that their visas allow them in Brazil. They are an illuminating couple. I felt like a kindred spirit with both of them.

When I walked onto the Casa grounds, I actually had a moment of lightheadedness. The feeling subsided shortly thereafter. From that moment throughout the rest of our journey in Abadiânia, my perceptions of everything, as well as my inner and outer being, felt otherworldly.

As we proceeded through the gate, we were guided over a ledge to speak with an interpreter. We told the interpreter what we wanted to ask or say to the entity when we would come before João. The interpreter wrote down our question or comment in the Portuguese language and then gave the paper back to us.

The morning and afternoon sessions at the Casa began at a specific time but ended at various times. On each Casa day, before the morning session began, João would come into a large Gathering Room and greet everyone. He would stand on a stage-like platform and share statements from his heart. I remember him saying, "I love all of you, my brothers and sisters. I wish all to be well and whole. I am not a healer; only God heals. I am just a man who has agreed to offer himself for God and the entities to use in their work." These words were interpreted for us. I remember feeling his love and kindness toward all of us. He was and is a very special man!

After João was finished speaking, two of his helpers held his hands while he allowed the entities to "incorporate" his body. Briefly summarizing the meaning of incorporate, João's body is brought to an unconscious state, while one entity, who is a loving being from another dimension of the spirit world, brings their spirit into the space of João's body. When this incorporation takes place, João's body shudders for a few seconds.

Once the incorporation has taken place, João either asks for a volunteer or chooses someone from the group to perform a "physical intervention" on. He will actually use a scalpel to cut something foreign out of the person's body (possibly a tumor), or he may use a scalpel to scrape their eye (for example, a cataract), or he may use forceps-type scissors, inserting them into someone's nostril. These procedures are intended to offer healing of some kind. João may work on a few people before starting the morning session in the Current Rooms. There are a couple of small TVs in this Gathering Room. These TVs run on a continual basis, showing recorded physical surgeries that he has performed. Dad and I were fascinated to witness this phenomenon up close.

The time had come for first timers, who had not yet gone before João, to line up. We proceeded through what is called the First Current Room. Many of the seats in this room were filled with people praying and meditating. Then we would continue to another room around the corner. This room was larger and triangular shaped. Many people were praying and meditating in this room as well. I peeked to the side of the person in front of me and could see João sitting in a chair at the head of the room.

The line moved fairly quickly as one person at a time handed their paper with a question or statement to the interpreter, once they came before the entity. When it was my turn, I handed my paper to the helper, with my statement, which read, "to be of greater service to my brothers and sisters." Our tour guide, Diana Rose, was up in front, guiding us with what to do after João replied to us. Diana said to me, "You are invited to sit in João's Current Room. This is a very special honor." She ushered me into a seat, where I closed my eyes (which is the rule when sitting in Current) and I cried for a few minutes. I was literally moved to tears with emotion. The energy in that room was INTENSE. I began to settle into what ended up to be a three-and-a-half-hour meditation session. I had never meditated for more than one hour at a time before. The time really flew and I felt engulfed in the most radiant feelings of peace and joy. Time seemed to stand still. I knew I was Present, but barely felt this reality that I was living in.

As the two weeks continued in Abadiânia, we had five more Casa days with morning and afternoon sessions. As I walked before João several more times, I was invited again to sit in his Current. One time when I walked before him, I was told to have what they call a "blessing." For this, you walk into yet another room, and prayers in Portuguese are offered. I was in this room for about ten minutes, then walked outside. I was told that this blessing was to help balance and cleanse us from any lower level energies we may have picked up. The blessing also helped align us to move forward with our life purpose. A woman that I had just met explained the above to me after we had walked outside of that room. I was overcome with emotion and began sobbing on her shoulder.

Dad and I each had a twin bed in our pousada room. We also had a private full bathroom to share. One evening, as we lay in our beds, quietly beginning to fall asleep, I experienced a most blessed healing. I began to feel a moving, like cutting sensation lengthwise about an inch below my belly button. I felt a sequence of this movement for about half a minute or so, then experienced the same sensation again. I felt no pain, just sensation. As this was occurring I shared it with my father. I just lay there with tears streaming down my face, quietly thanking the entities for the healing that they were offering me.

During the Casa days of our trip, many and most people had spiritual interventions (or surgeries). Many people had more than one. I did not have any that were officially prescribed by João, but rather the unofficial surgery (or intervention) in my bed and while in Current. I spoke with a few other people who had surgeries in their room as well. One woman felt totally exhausted after her Casa visits. She would leave after the sessions and go back to her room, where she would sleep until the next morning. A man stayed in his pousada during all the downtime that we had, feeling inspired to write an album of songs. He did so, and it was a beautiful little treasure.

Ron Roth and João truly felt themselves to be kindred spirit-brothers. Ron was a little older then João, but their birthdays were only one day apart. One evening at our pousada, a grand birthday celebration was held for the two of them. João and his wife joined us as we gathered together. There was a very large cake and a happy birthday song and, of course, a speech from Ron. It was a wonderful experience for these two beloved men and all who were part of this event.

We learned that some local people from Abadiânia recited one hour of the rosary in Portuguese at the Casa every evening. Anyone could attend. Dad and I went a few times, and it was so very beautiful to experience. The other nights I preferred to stay outside on the grounds of the pousada. One evening after dinner, many from our pousada left to attend the rosary while I decided to stick around in order to be in Ron's presence. Ten of us sat around in a little circle while Ron began a very casual conversation with us. This was an extremely rare opportunity for which I felt blessed beyond measure. Ron's words to us were so loving, empowering, and sweet. He was funny and witty, which I so loved about him. At the end of this informal teaching and sharing, he said to us, "When I leave you, you will do this work." I truly felt in my heart that this was true. I can only speak for myself, but Ron was my greatest inspiration for beginning my own healing ministry.

At the end of the two weeks in Brazil, I felt transformed yet again. I knew that my life would never be completely the same again. Coming back to the United States was a difficult transition time for me. After being in the elevated energy of the Casa area, it took me a few weeks to transition back to the denser energy of everyday reality. For a while I was easily overwhelmed by long, tedious tasks and prolonged conversations. My family sensed my challenges in integrating back into what was once a comfortable reality. I was grateful for their understanding.

Chapter 10

Stepping out into Ministry

In April 2006, I attended what was to be the last Healing Intensive that Ron Roth led. At this retreat Ron focused on sharing the lives of three women who, in their lifetimes, were spiritual healing evangelists: Maria Woodworth-Etter, Aimee Semple McPherson, and Kathryn Kuhlman. Ron encouraged us to read about the lives of these women. He wanted us to really feel the passion and energy behind their ministries. I feel very blessed to have attended one of Kathryn Kuhlman's "Miracle Services" with my family in Rhode Island when I was just thirteen years old.

Although these women were born-again Christians in the traditional sense (while I am not), the passion and love behind their messages, as well as their devotion to God, touched me very deeply. I had already begun to feel empowered by Spirit's messages through Ron. Reading about the works of these women was icing on the cake. Regarding born-again believers, in my eyes Joel Osteen is a Fundamental Christian with a Unity message. I find his words to be loving, kind, and greatly empowering. He is also very easy on the eye. I have learned from many great teachers and don't necessarily adopt everything they say, just what resonates with me. So as they say, "take the best and leave the rest." Our faith and truth are very individual.

In June 2006 I began to feel some restlessness. My soul yearned to express more deeply in a new way. Just one month earlier, I had begun attending Unity of Greater Hartford. Reverend Raymond Shea (no relation to me) was the residing minister in a beautiful new church in South Windsor, Connecticut. From the start, Unity was home for me. I still can't believe that after only one month of attending services there, at Spirit's urging, I called the church and made an appointment to speak with Reverend Raymond about my new passion of ministry. As I walked into his office, I remember feeling very nervous, as I was not sure what I was going to say and I definitely was not sure of what his reaction would be. He had been seeing me come to the church every week for a month, but we did not know each other well.

As I sat down, I decided to speak from my heart. I told him I had felt guided to offer a monthly healing time at church. I could offer a message, some prayers, and hands-on healing. I mentioned I was a certified Reiki practitioner. Our conversation lasted no more than fifteen minutes. He said, "Yes," and he was excited for me to do this. He asked me to begin in September. I left that meeting feeling like a whole new world had opened up for me. For the next six years I offered monthly healing prayer time services at Unity of Greater Hartford.

Chapter 11

My Great Heartache

In August 2006, Ron Roth had a stroke. As well as many others, I was very distraught at this news. I began sending Ron a dozen roses each month. Doing so made me feel that might brighten his day. I felt so grateful to give something to him after all he had given to me. Ron's business partner and now President of Celebrating Life Ministries, Paul Funfsinn, would call me with Ron on the phone and thank me for the flowers. I loved hearing both of their voices. Although it would be a year and a half before I was to see Ron and Paul again, I continued listening to Ron's teachings via cassettes and CDs.

Yearning for a spiritual adventure, I found out about a yoga retreat center in Vanderbilt, Michigan, called Song of the Morning. This center was founded by Oliver Black, a direct disciple of Paramhansa Yogananda. I registered to spend four days at the center at the end of May 2007. My dad wanted to meet a spiritual author named Marianne Johnston who lived there, so he took the trip with me. The retreat was four glorious days of meditating in the amazingly powerful ashram room. It was contemplative with walks through wooded paths. A separate path was designated for each of the four masters honored there: Paramhansa Yogananda, Sri Yukteswar, Sri Aurobindo, and Jesus. The first one hundred feet or so of the Jesus path was laid in naturally growing green moss. It felt like velvet on my bare feet. These walks were very sacred. Dad and I felt the Presence of the "cloud of witnesses," Ron's phrase for spirit helpers. They were all around us. We got lost pretty deep into the woods on one of the paths, but felt no fear, knowing guidance would come. Before we knew it, we were shown the way back to where we had come.

The meals in the dining area were vegetarian and fabulous. People from the area could pay a nominal fee and dine there. One evening a young Indian boy and his grandmother came for dinner. They sat across from Dad and me.

The boy was about ten years old. This young boy seemed so present in the moment that he was not aware of things happening around him. He became very fixated on me. He began saying to me, "I love you." After a few times, in a motherly affectionate way, I said, "I love you too." A few minutes later the young boy and his grandmother stood up and moved away from the table. Dad and I got up as well. The young boy came over and gave me a big hug. He let go of me and then hugged me again. He did this three or four times. His grandmother walked near me and said, "He only hugs Amma like that." I was so humbled that he could show me love in that way and feel my love in return. I look back fondly on this most free-spirited, joyful adventure.

The fall of 2007, a Celebrating Life Ministry Intensive was planned in Illinois. All thought Ron would be well enough to lead it. This turned out not to be the case, as he suffered more mini-strokes, which caused a setback for him. I was really feeling the need to be near him, but knew this was not possible, since I was not a close personal friend. I knew Paul was caring for Ron at his home. I decided to have my own four-day retreat of prayer, rest and relaxation at the lodge where the Intensive would have taken place. It made me feel closer to Ron, to be in the same state and only a half-hour from his home.

I called Trina Funfsinn, Paul's sister-in-law, just to say, "Hi." Trina and I had become friends, and it felt good to talk with her about Ron at times. To my surprise, Trina spoke with Paul and mentioned my possibly visiting with Ron. Paul agreed and Trina, who lived near Ron, brought me to his home the next day. That day was, and always will be, one of the highlights of my life. As many people know, I love to hug and gave Ron very many hugs and kisses when I saw him. I had the most wonderful visit, talking and sharing stories with him. I was, and still continue to be, so grateful for that time of closeness with him. In many ways Ron was like a father to me. He taught with love and firmness. He modeled for me "Living in Grace." I aspired to be in that state as well. After his stroke, his softer, gentler side was revealed, which made him just about the sweetest man alive.

Chapter 12

The Work at Hand

I was feeling the call to journey back to Brazil, but only for one week this time. The normal time to be with your tour group was two weeks. I felt, however, that two weeks was too long to be away from my daughter, who was seventeen at the time. Dad wanted to go back to Abadiânia as well. So off we went in April 2008.

I didn't have any official spiritual interventions (or surgeries) on this trip either. This freed me up to be of service to the others in our group. All of the other people had more than one intervention in the two weeks they were there. I was able to bring people meals to their pousada room. The protocol after an intervention is for the person to spend twenty-four hours resting in their room. Many people revealed that they felt exhausted and weak after the surgery.

This trip was a wonderful opportunity for meeting new brothers and sisters in our group, as well as others at the Casa. One of the women in our group was a nun. One day while we were having lunch together with a few other people at our table, this sweet nun asked me how I prayed, what my beliefs were, and how I stayed so joyful. The beautiful thing was that she was a nun who had traveled to Abadiânia to be in the presence of João for healing. The fact that she was open enough to be there assured me that I didn't have to worry that she might judge me for giving up my Catholic faith when I was nineteen – not that what she thought really would have bothered me anyway. As I began to answer her questions, she began to cry. She put her hands over her face and began sobbing. She told me that my voice, the words I spoke, and my very presence moved her to tears. I shared with her that I have said to other people, when they told me of similar feelings, that "it is Spirit speaking through me." There is a Christian song whose words and passion really move me. The lyrics say, "Let them see You in me. Let them hear You when I speak, and let them feel You when I sing." I know that through our spirit we can all have the ability to affect one another in positive, healing ways. This can manifest through us from our love and devotion to Source, as well as our trust and faith in ourselves. "You will do as I have done and greater things than these shall you do," said Jesus. Through my service in Brazil I came home with an even greater desire to help myself and others.

Over the next year I spent time with a few people who were entering the transitional phase of their lives. Having no formal training in counseling, I was amazed how Spirit led me to the appropriate words to say, offering people hope, comfort, and resolution with their lives. I was open, and intuitively knew what each person wanted me to offer them. All but one wanted hands-on healing each time I met with them. I sometimes shared Bible verses, prayers, and positive evaluations of their lives. They enjoyed my company and I enjoyed theirs as well. They looked forward to sharing with me some of their family experiences and hardships. I knew Spirit was using me as a set of ears and as a comforter to help them find self-love and to ease them into peaceful transition. I was there to help banish their fears of the next phase of their evolving spiritual journey. I am very grateful to have known all of them. They left a joyful mark on my life and left this earth plane with peace and dignity.

Ron Roth, being ill, passed the torch on to his successor, Paul Funfsinn, who became President of Celebrating Life Ministries. Since Ron was no longer able to lead the ministry, Paul led his first retreat in May 2008. Paul was excited to carry on Ron's legacy and begin a new one of his own. It was very exciting to have the retreats begin again. Ron came to the retreats as well and made an appearance at some of the sessions. I made chocolate chip cookies for Ron, as he used to tell the retreat attendees how much he loved them. On the first day of the retreat I gave Paul the tin of cookies for Ron. Paul told me that I could give Ron the cookies myself in their hotel room. I was very excited to do so. Ron was so happy to eat some cookies right away. I was able to have some pictures taken of the both of us together. We spoke for a few minutes. It was truly wonderful, since I had not seen him in a long time.

Paul was amazing at the retreats. He had never planned to be Ron's successor, but Spirit and Ron had counted on this. Paul was now ready to walk this path. At the retreat, Paul spoke to the group from his heart. It was like coming home to the core part of the family for those of us who had stood by and waited for this to happen.

Paul offered a healing service the first evening. When he touched people who were lined up, many fell back and were caught by a catcher to "lay in the Spirit." This was the start of Paul's ministry. We had another retreat in Illinois in the fall of 2008 as well.

As I mentioned previously, I am so grateful for the love and devotion of this ministry and those who gather at our retreats. We are Spiritual family, guiding and supporting one another to keep growing, keep sharing the love, and never give up on our dreams and desires. We believe through intention, our desires become our reality.

Paul has loved and supported me through all my opportunities of being in service. He too has been a father figure for me over these past eleven years.

Chapter 13

The Final Goodbye

Paul decided to hold off on leading a spring retreat in 2009. For a while it had seemed as though Ron would walk again, but now his condition worsened. On June 1, 2009, Ron made his transition back home to the Spirit world. I was devastated. I flew to Illinois to attend the services and funeral. I cried until there were no tears left. I trusted that his journey was over on this earth plane, but I just couldn't believe it or understand it. For a full month, every time I began meditating, I cried. I felt sorry for myself. I felt his loss deeply because I had felt closer to Ron than to anyone else I knew who had passed away. I thought of myself as his disciple and of him as my guru.

This process was a good lesson for me. It taught me to never again become so attached to a partner, other family member, friend, or guru. I am grateful for this lesson in non-attachment. I am human though, and now and then some feelings of attachment with a person may creep in, and I have to work at regaining my understanding that they may be in my life for just a season or two.

The services for Ron were a beautiful celebration of his life and service to humanity. I shared with Ron a love of winter with fireplace fires, yellow roses, food, sweets, and Christmas time.

At the end of the luncheon following Ron's funeral, Paul and I hugged goodbye. We were both crying when he whispered in my ear, "I would like to profess you as a monk in the Spirit of Peace Monastic Community." Becoming a monk meant agreeing to spend some time each day in prayer, holding all of humanity in love and light. Paul also shared with me that I was the last one Ron had chosen to be a monk before his condition worsened. I was so moved and touched by our entire conversation, and I graciously accepted the invitation. Lucky for me with this type of Monastic, there is no requirement to be celibate, for that would not have flowed with my life.

Ron was my greatest spiritual teacher in this life, as he brought me to a heightened understanding of many spiritual principles and ways of being. He will live in my heart forever. He is always there for comfort and guidance when I need him. He used to say "Sometimes God takes the good from us, in order to give us the best." He will always be an inspirational, driving force in my life and ministry.

Paul led the October 2009 retreat for CLM. It was just four short months after Ron's transition. Time and prayer were helping to mend my broken heart. Many tears were shed by all during this weekend retreat in remembrance and gratitude for all of Ron's love, teachings, and healings. I was professed a monk at this retreat. The ceremony was very moving and emotional for me. I felt Ron's presence around me, which was very comforting.

Our musical leader Kathy had emailed me several weeks earlier asking for song requests for my ceremony. One of the songs I chose was "You Light Up My Life." I remembered seeing Debby Boone in person when I was nineteen years old. She sang that song in praise to our Beloved. Dad and Mom had brought me to her concert. Her father, Pat Boone, sang as well. I wasn't thrilled to go initially, but that song has stayed in my heart all these years. The second song I chose was "Follow Me" by John Denver. This song was also played at my wedding. The third song I chose was played at the last Intensive that Ron led in April 2006. I can still remember huddling around him on that last day. We were honoring Ron for his life and work. The song was "You Raise Me Up." As I mentioned previously, I have always felt that through our Beloved, Ron raised me up to walk fearlessly through any seeming obstacle, with poise, confidence, and unending love for our Creator, myself, and all brothers and sisters.

As this last song was played during my ceremony, I began to cry. I got up from my chair and walked over to Paul. I embraced him, as we began sobbing in honor of our Great Servant and Teacher, Ron. Shortly after the ceremony, Paul called my father over to congratulate me. Dad hugged and kissed me, and then turned to the group and said, "This is my beloved daughter, in whom I am well pleased." I was grateful and blessed to have my dad there, in good health. He was eighty-one years old at the time.

My father and I have shared many fun and exciting spiritual adventures together. We have been each other's companions through travel and spiritual exploration, as our spouses do not pursue exercising a spiritual life. We do honor our spouses, knowing that everyone pursues what is right and perfect for them at any given time.

Chapter 14

The Greatest Shift and the Feminine Presence

Reverend Ed Townley signed on as our new Senior Minister at Unity of Greater Hartford in the summer of 2009. Reverend Raymond Shea had relocated in 2008. We had an interim Minister, Reverend Phil Smedstad, for a year and a half before Reverend Ed came.

To me, Ed was in some ways an extension of Ron Roth. I was inspired by Ed's speaking, charisma, and vitality. Ed taught "Bible Alive" at Unity on Sunday mornings from 9 to 10 a.m. I eagerly looked forward to this informal group of sharing old and new spiritual ideas, which expanded our spiritual knowledge. I was always looking for new things of interest on the horizon. What I had known about the Bible up to this point, I had credited to Ron's teachings. Ed expanded it even further, taking interpretive Bible studies to a whole new level. I was intrigued, inspired, and not afraid to speak up and voice my opinion. I felt Ed and I developed a nice friendship. I also made great friendships with the fifteen or so of us who regularly attended the class.

In October 2009, I felt nudged by Spirit to begin a monthly meditation group in my home. Dad and I, as well as five other friends from "Bible Alive," were eager to experience the Presence of the Spirit at our meetings. We are still going strong to this day. Our meditation time is very powerful. We send our collective energy out to all people, places, and circumstances in need. After our time in meditation, we have hospitality and sharing of spiritual conversation or view DVDs. I am grateful for our time together.

The fall of 2009 was my sixth time volunteering to "serve in Current" when John of God came to the Omega Institute in Rhinebeck, New York. It has been a beautiful honor to be part of this service team. Each year it became a greater blessing. Those of us who love to facilitate and serve, understand and feel great fulfillment within our soul for all the opportunities that come before us in service to humanity. I continued to serve in Current when John of God came to Omega Institute in 2011 and 2014. I was honored to be present in 2011 when Wayne Dyer was told by the entities that his healing was complete and he was cured of an "incurable" form of leukemia.

In my own healing practice I had begun getting feedback from folks who had private energy healing/coaching sessions with me, others who attended my services at Unity and other venues, and some I laid hands on at CLM retreats. One common element in their feedback was that they felt love and comfort when I laid hands on them. They felt a feminine healing presence around them. Sometimes they would describe this as "Marian" or "Angelic." Some described seeing beautiful colors or spirit beings, and became emotional during these times, weeping uncontrollably. What I shared with them was that for some time, at the end of my daily power walks, I would walk over and visit with the statue of Mary, which stood in the parking lot of a Catholic church next to my street. I cannot remember what drew me to her the very first time, except my memory of Mary's statue and her Presence at my church when I was a child. I remember that my visits to the statue near my home began in the winter time and snow flurries were falling softly all about her. As I looked up at her face, I felt a great sense of peace. As I looked above her head, off to the sides of her head, and down to her shoulders, I began to see white spirited figures. In this moment, love permeated my being and senses. I felt "stilled" in the moment.

As my visits became more regular with the essence of Mary, she revealed to me the idea of taking a sacred journey to Medjugorje. A few years earlier, I had been contemplating the idea of going there. Ron Roth had journeyed there several times and spoke of his amazing experiences. The main reason I did not go was that my husband felt fear with the idea of my going.

Mary shared with me that by spending time in Medjugorje, even more of the "feminine essence" would flow through me, offering love, compassion, understanding, and healing for people. So I continued my visits at the statue. I regularly saw spirit beings around Mary's statue, and I continued to hear the invitation to go to Medjugorje. I was assured it would be safe for me to take that sacred journey.

I was ready and I felt convinced, but the hard part was breaking the news to my husband. Bob's first words were, "Can't you please stay in the United States? How can you tell me you want to go to Bosnia?" All I could tell him was, "I have to go, and I will be safe." He reluctantly said, "I know I can't stop you." The next day I searched the Internet and found a United States tour leader to go with and booked my trip for March 2010.

I called Paul Funfsinn, President of CLM, the next week and shared the news. He looked into going there as well. He rounded up a small group of CLM folks and booked their trip for the same time, using the same United States tour guide as I had.

I flew to Germany on my own. The rest of the journey, I was with Paul and the other folks in the group. The story of Medjugorje is that in the 1980's Mary appeared regularly to six children on Apparition Hill. She sent messages of peace and love for the children. They were to share these messages with people of the area. There was a war being fought in the area when she first appeared. Mary's messages were addressing that issue. Some people believed the children and others did not. Three of the children, now adults, still receive messages to this day, either on a daily, monthly, or yearly basis.

We arrived safely in a quaint town where the apparitions occurred. We stayed in the home of a woman whose sister was one of the visionaries. I was grateful to stay at the end of town, only a block from Apparition Hill, where the visions took place.

Our local tour guide brought us to a few different places. One was the center of the village. Many shops adorned the streets, offering many sacred objects from the area, as well as many religious items. I bought a pendant of Immaculate Mary at a jewelry store.

Two churches stood in the center of town. An outdoor "Stations of the Cross" walk was accessible for anyone to follow. There were outdoor confessionals, which I found interesting. As a child I had to be almost dragged, kicking and screaming, to a confessional. From the time I was a little girl, I felt that I could communicate with God by myself and didn't need to do this through a priest. I also believed that God loved me. Pretty odd for a Catholic child, I realize. Outside and behind one of the churches there stood a man-made metal statue of Jesus. He wore only the wrap around his waist for clothing. The phenomenon with this statue was that a drop of water came out of its side every five seconds or so. The builders of the statue have never been able to figure out why this happened, or how to stop it. Some people filled small containers to bring home, feeling that it was holy water from the wound of Jesus. I must admit I let a little drip on my hand and dabbed it on myself.

On another outing, we hiked up to Cross Mountain. It is about 1700 feet high. Our group shared in reciting the Stations of the Cross on the way up. It wasn't my favorite thing to do as a child or at this time as well, but I went along with it. The view from the top of the mountain was breathtaking. An extremely large cross adorned the peak.

Another wonderful experience was visiting an orphanage. We were not allowed to see the children in their classrooms though. These children were cared for by Catholic nuns. In the gift shop there were several clay-molded and painted items that the children had made. They were being sold for a nominal fee. I bought a little girl Angel. She is painted white with gold wings. She stands on a table in my sanctuary now.

My favorite part of this trip was climbing up to Apparition Hill. Each morning and evening the group went to Mass. I went to Mass one morning when Paul was officiating as a Deacon. I attended the larger church one time for a healing service. All the other times, when the group went into town for Mass, I walked up the rocks to Apparition Hill. On top there is a beautiful white statue of Mary as she looked when she appeared to the children in the late 1980's. This is the most beautiful statue of Mary I have ever seen. She has one hand on her heart and the other outstretched to humanity.

Most of my time on Apparition Hill was spent alone. March was a cool time in Medjugorje. We wore heavier coats on most of the days. It was a very quiet time to visit. As I sat with Mary each time I visited, I felt her Presence most powerfully. I opened my heart to all her love and surrendered to my purpose. I was open to all that she was, moving through me. Her essence was so comforting and genuine.

One overcast day when I was alone with Mary, I had an amazing surprise. Rain began to fall, so I put on my poncho. And then it began hailing, luckily not golf-ball size. Thunder boomed very loudly, but there was no lightening.

I sat through all of this with joyful tears running down my face. She was speaking to me. Mary was making a proclamation. She was telling me that I was ready to hold the feminine energy and that many would be touched by this. I felt her essence penetrate my being and I knew the truth of her love for me and all of humanity. All I could feel was "Hallelujah, praise God from whom all blessings flow!" I was ready to move forward with my purposeful service. After that very day, my journey in Medjugorje felt complete.

Chapter 15

Grounding and Regrouping

After my journey to Medjugorje, my work deepened with the people at the monthly Unity service in which I offered hands-on healing. I began moving through each day of life with even more of a grateful heart for all that I had received. I did notice though, that I was having a hard time staying grounded. I was experiencing living on an ethereal level a lot of the time, and it was becoming increasingly difficult for me to function in "this world." The feeling for me was like having one foot in the spirit world and the other one on earth. That sounds wonderful, but it can be very challenging. I attended the spring 2010 CLM retreat, which was only two weeks after returning from Medjugorje. Spirit was asking more of me in terms of expanding my work. I was told, "You and your husband have a great relationship, but you are being called to greater work." I had been feeling a restlessness but wasn't sure of my new direction. I flowed through the summer months without much change.

I attended the fall CLM retreat and broke my ankle three days after returning home. While walking down a street in Maine, I backed into broken curb chunks, and down into a little dip. I thought my ankle was just sprained, as I didn't hear a pop. I hopped around for five days and then had my ankle x-rayed. It was broken. I declined a cast to the doctor's dismay. I settled for a Velcro® boot and crutches. The doctor told me if the bone moved, I would need surgery. He told me that it would be eight weeks before I would walk. I told him, "Four weeks."

For four weeks I spent my days on the couch. I had to take the time off from my part-time childcare provider job. I stopped delivering Meals on Wheels. I stopped my helping at a local soup kitchen. I took pause from my private healing sessions with clients. I had to cancel only one of my monthly services at Unity and one monthly meditation group that I was part of.

Every morning Bob helped me pack my food in the cooler for the day. I parked myself on the couch in my family room. I only got up to use the bathroom and to sit in another room for a while, in front of the window with the sun beaming through. With my sedentary living, I gained six pounds in four weeks. I continued to eat all the great foods I normally do to keep my strength up. I was put on the prayer list at Unity Church. Each day I undid the Velcro boot, touched my foot, and gave my ankle its healing. I journaled and thanked Spirit for this opportunity to regroup and ground myself. I felt in no way like a victim. I trusted that every experience has value and lessons built into it. We can be bitter or we can be better from our experiences. It's our choice.

I was x-rayed after two weeks. The doctor was surprised to see some new bone growth so soon. Two weeks later the x-ray revealed that, to the doctor's amazement, I was ready to walk. He said to me, "I don't know what you did, but you have healed faster than anyone from ages twenty-five to eighty-five." I told him that it was faith, trust, and prayer that sped up the healing process for me.

This truly was a blessed opportunity for me to find balance. It was also nice to see how well Bob took care of me. I had to go up and down my long flight of stairs on my bottom each day. Bob helped me in and out of the bath chair each night. He had to wash all the dishes and clean the house. It was a great time of appreciation and growth for both of us.

For the past several summers, Bob and I had been taking four to five days in the summer to vacation in Vermont. I have loved Vermont since I was a child, visiting Santa's Land and Basketville. I am not partial to intense summer heat. The weather in Vermont is always ten to twelve degrees cooler than in northern Connecticut.

In the spring of 2011, I was talking with Bob about finding a second home for us as a mountain retreat. He was open to searching online. We found a Vermont realtor who chose some homes for us to look at, and we went to Vermont. There was a home online, small and quaint, that we both liked. I had asked to see it last. I was thinking that if I liked it, then I wouldn't want to see the other homes. The homes we looked at were nice but didn't speak to me. When we walked into the last home, I said to our realtor, "This is it!" We bought this home three years ago. It is quaint, rustic, comfortable, and easy to clean. We have a spectacular view of Haystack Mountain and a decent view of Mount Snow. We are across from Mount Snow, the ski mountain, and it is quiet here. When I am in Vermont, I feel a bit closer to heaven on earth. I feel light and free, as my spirit soars to new heights. I love my home in Connecticut as well. We have great neighbors and beautiful woods behind our home. Just last week a tagged mother bear and baby bear passed through my backyard. I couldn't believe that I had yet to see a bear in Vermont, but saw them in Connecticut.

You know the saying that goes "home is where the heart is." I truly feel I can bring my heart wherever I go and it feels like home to me.

Chapter 16

Longing for More

During the first few months of 2012, a restlessness began in me again. I loved spending time in Vermont with Bob, snowshoeing, and fixing up our place together. My spirit, however, was yearning for more work. In July, Reverend Ed asked me to speak in his place during a Sunday service. He was going to be out of town. I eagerly said, "Yes," but was nervous at the same time. I put together what I would speak about and included my healing story as well. I received good feedback from people. They felt my talk was light, airy, and refreshing. I took that as a compliment.

That same summer, the energy began to become more intensified during my monthly healing services at Unity of Greater Hartford. My body even began to shudder and shake more when offering hands-on healing. I asked Spirit to guide me in understanding this. I was informed that I was experiencing energy surges. When a new surge moved in with equal or greater intensity, my body's reaction was to shake. I was guided to breathe through this to keep from shaking. I am grateful to say that it worked, and I continued to breathe this way for a month or two until my body adjusted.

Along with my friend Jim, I registered to attend the Unity Eastern Regional Conference. Our church was sponsoring the conference at the Hilton Hotel in Hartford, Connecticut. Jim and I were to set up the prayer room. I was still feeling the restlessness that had been a part of me since March. These restless feelings were similar to how I felt before approaching Reverend Raymond Shea with the idea to facilitate healing services at Unity of Greater Hartford. I was hopeful Spirit might reveal some guidance to me at the conference.

The conference "meet and greet" was Monday evening. It was really fun speaking with folks from the other Unity churches in the region. On Tuesday, Bhante Wimala (a Buddhist monk) enlightened us on his work. He and others from his order offer a listening ear, comfort, and prayer to people in prison. He shared with us of their strict diet of mainly rice and beans. These monks spend a lot of time in prayer and silence each day. Bhante spoke of how his brother had been brought to this monk's order as a child. An elder of the order saw Bhante and said, "He's the one who is supposed to live this life." Bhante's parents agreed and he's been there ever since. He shared with us that he was not happy for a while. He had been a very active and restless child. The ways of the monks (being calm and peaceful) were a difficult challenge and adjustment for him. Bhante was a delightful speaker. He imbued a calm demeanor with a fun sense of humor.

On Tuesday evening we had an "open mic" night. People could sign up to sing, dance, or offer anything of talent that they chose. Andrea Paquin, from Unity of Greater Hartford at that time, sang some songs from her album. She was fabulous as always. The Unity of Greater Hartford Choir sang for us. I had the opportunity to meet Reverend Justin Epstein from the Unity Center of New York City that evening. Spirit would later reveal to me the idea of Reverend Justin and me offering a healing service together. After discussing this with him, we booked the date of December 30, 2012, to facilitate a healing service together in his church in New York City. I was a bit nervous and didn't quite know what to expect regarding the amount of interest and attendance. I knew in my heart, though, that the energy and vibration around us were very powerful.

As it turned out, around one hundred people joined us for the service. My father Joe and sister Sandy took the train into New York City for the service that day. Reverend Ed Townley, along with friends Terrie and John, attended as well. Andrea Paquin, Elise Arsenault, and their band provided the soul-filled music for the service. Once the music began, my nervousness left and I melted as one with Spirit. When I got up to offer a prayer written by Ron Roth, my entire body was vibrating. I left my body and felt Ron's presence reciting the prayer through me. This was one of the most magical and memorable experiences of my life.

Reverend Justin and I offered hands-on healing to every person in attendance. When I received feedback from folks on that day and on subsequent days, and even months later, some shared with me that they felt a change, a shift, and somehow lighter. They were touched in some way. Thank you, Beloved Spirit!

Reverend Justin and I offered one more service together in April 2013. This service was very powerful as well. I am grateful for both of these opportunities to be of service at his Unity Center.

I was feeling very empowered at this point in my life. I continued offering healing services. One was at my home and I facilitated two at the First Congregational Church in my town. Andrea and Elise provided glorious music for these events. I facilitated healing services at the Atma Center and at Spirit Expressing in subsequent months. My dear friend, Jan Craft, shared her amazing harp melodies with us during these events. She has since moved to Chicago, and I was grateful for her love and support as I began to spread my wings and fly.

I collaborated with my dear friend and fellow CLM attendee Reverend Kat Katsanis-Semel. We held two healing services together at the Meta Center in New York City. The love and powerful energy that came through were felt by all who attended. Reverend Ed Townley and I collaborated on a most heart-felt service at the Meta Center as well.

These times were a bit challenging for Bob and me. I was becoming more independent and busy with my work. It led us through some arguments, disagreements, and growing pains. This is all part of relationships and moving forward with the work that is yours to do. I was fair and straight with Bob, sharing that I would not give up my Spirit-led work. I would continue to grow and share my work whenever aligned opportunities might arise for me. He ultimately agreed and turned his fear of losing me over to the universe. This was very brave of him to do so, releasing control and attachment, and allowing our marriage to play out for both of our highest truth and evolution. I am very proud of him for taking this huge leap of faith, with the understanding that this present moment is all there truly is.

Reverend Ed Townley left Unity of Greater Hartford at the end of 2012. He reignited Spirit Expressing, a soul-filled gathering of "truth seekers." These gatherings offer deep discussions and ponderings on the teachings of Jesus and other great masters, whose universal message was LOVE for all.

Chapter 17

My Most Holy and Sacred Journey

As the summer of 2013 arrived, I began spiritually preparing myself for what was to be the most holy of experiences in my lifetime thus far. I was given the opportunity to join Paul Funfsinn and fifteen other friends from the CLM community to literally walk in the footsteps of the Great Master, Jesus.

In my meditations throughout the summer, I had been praying to Jesus that I might feel his energy and Presence throughout the trip and especially at the sacred sites. I felt so prepared and so ready for this pilgrimage. Bob was nervous and fearful for my safety. I assured him that I would be fine. I felt very protected.

October 2, 2013 finally arrived. This was the day I would leave for Israel. I was so excited for the adventure ahead of me. Bob planned business in New Jersey, so he could drive me to the Newark Airport. We had a direct flight to Tel Aviv. As I turned to walk into the airport, Bob's last words to me were, "Please come back to me." I said, "Don't worry; I will."

I checked my bag, went through security, and went to our gate. It was enclosed with security all around. I didn't see anyone from our group through the glass, so I waited outside. Before too long others joined me.

In the evening on the plane, a group of Orthodox Jewish men were not far from where I sat. They began their time of prayer. I was fascinated to witness their steadfast devotion. They weren't concerned with who may be judging them or annoyed by them. Their focus was devotion to our one Beloved. No matter what faith, it is the same Source with different names according to thy faith. The memory of them praying will always be with me.

We landed safely in Tel Aviv, boarded a privately chartered bus just for our group, and headed to Nazareth. Thankfully I was able to sleep quite a bit on the flight, as we went right into our day. I brought a change of clothes in my carry-on suitcase, since the forecast for Nazareth called for temperatures in the 80's.

We stayed in a kibbutz, a small hotel, on the Sea of Galilee, for our four days in Nazareth. The sea view from the dock was spectacular. I collected many rocks from the shore. During our stay in Nazareth, we toured the home where Jesus took part at the Wedding Feast. This was where Jesus turned water into wine, so the parents of the bride would not be embarrassed at having run out. One of my friends on the trip, Kathy, stayed with me in the lower part of the home for a bit. We placed our hands on the Plexiglas® that encased part of an area. Kathy and I looked at one another with tear-filled eyes as we felt intense energy in there. I was able to reach my hand over and take a few small pebbles for souvenirs.

While in Nazareth, we went to a museum that housed an old fishing boat that dated back to the time that Jesus lived. This was so awesome to see. Whether this boat was from the fishermen/disciples, we do not know. I can tell you that the energy from this vessel was of high magnitude. For a period of time as I gazed at it, I felt spellbound.

Then we went out on a replica of a boat from Jesus's time period. It was quite an adventure to be out on the Sea of Galilee! Paul and Virginia offered a service of sorts on the boat, which was very beautiful. We sang many songs together and danced as a group. It was a delightful time for all.

While in Nazareth, we went to the site of the Beatitudes. During Jesus's time, this was a banana field. Our tour guide, Gershon, shared with us that Jesus would have been standing at the bottom of the hill speaking up to the crowd for the best voice delivery. The area at the hill was fenced in a few years earlier because some tourists were destroying the hill.

Our next stop was the Dead Sea, a most incredible phenomenon. My friend Penny and I wanted to soak in the sea after we checked into our hotel for the night. The rest of the group had planned to go over in the morning. Penny and I had about an hour before dark, once we made our way to the beach area. She had been to Israel the year before and had floated in the sea, but I was a rookie. I put my hair up in a high bun, so as not to let the sulfur get all through it. The water was a very comfortable temperature. It's amazing how you can float on your back with your legs up in the air and stay in that position. This is because the sulfur/mineral content of the water keeps you buoyant.

There were very few people in the sea. It was amazingly calm and peaceful. Even Penny and I, who would often laugh a lot together, suddenly stilled ourselves, allowing the peacefulness of the moment.

The next day we were bused to the Jordan River. This is an area that is very commercialized. We stopped by just to see it. Gershon then took us to an area of the Jordan River believed to be in the vicinity of where John the Baptist had baptized people. This is felt to be where John had baptized Jesus as well. Paul offered to baptize us in the river. I had been looking forward to this moment. We purchased white above-the-knee, short-sleeved robes. We wore our bathing suits under them. From the time I put the robe over my bathing suit, I began sobbing. I couldn't stop. We proceeded down to a deck by the water. I was so "present" in the moment that I didn't realize until afterward that the water was thick, green and murky. It looked like water that alligators would live in.

Our group stood in a circle and held hands. Paul offered a few prayers. After this we began singing some familiar CLM songs. I continued sobbing through all of it. I was overcome with emotion and gratitude for this devotional opportunity.

My turn arrived, and Rick helped me down the steps into the water. Tuan was on one side of me and Paul on the other. At this point my sobbing had turned to full-out crying. If it hadn't been a spiritual moment, I might have been embarrassed. Paul said to me, "Let me know when you're ready, Shari." I looked up to the heavens and said, "Beloved, I am yours completely. Take me and do your will. I give my life to you in service." Paul blessed me and then he and Tuan dunked me. Rick helped me out of the water. This was it! No matter what might happen in my life, my devotion was to God above all else. Now my mission was sealed.

I knew that when Paul dunked me in that water, the re-immersion experience would be the "ultimate surrender and giving of my life to my Beloved Source." I am teary just remembering these most precious moments.

After everyone was baptized, we headed to Jerusalem. The temperatures were in the 70's, very comfortable. We visited what had been the disciple Peter's home. Jesus went to this home to heal Peter's mother, who had been ill. The church was built above part of the ruins of the home. We were told that all the darker gray stones were originals from all of the sacred sites where Jesus had been. Wrought iron fencing prevented us from walking up to the stones. I was drawn to a particular area and stood there for several minutes. I began weeping, as I felt Jesus's Presence all around. I looked over to one of my friends in the group, Rita. She was standing in the same area that I was, just around the corner. The look on her face revealed to me that she felt the same Presence as well.

We visited the site of the Transfiguration where Jesus appeared to his disciples and after he had resurrected. We were able to walk right down to the area of water where archaeologists believe this occurred. Our tour guide, Gershon, said, "Fifty feet this way or fifty feet that way.... It is an approximation." If so inclined we were able to walk barefoot, wading in the rocky water. I collected seven rocks from the water as I waded around. A small church was built at the beach area on this site. Inside was a large stone, thought to possibly be the one that Jesus used when he fixed the fish breakfast for the disciples.

On our walk down to the site of the Transfiguration, we saw two outdoor chapels along the side. After our visit to the site, Paul facilitated a beautiful communion service. It was powerful, moving me to tears.

We went to the site where Jesus healed the blind man. I took one two-inch stone from this site. Today I keep the stone in the small wooden chalice that held my wine from one of our communion services in Israel. They are in my sanctuary.

The site where Jesus healed the crippled man at Bethesda was amazing. There were so many cement tub areas and slabs. It must have been an array of pools. There was a church just across the way and most of the group went there. My friend Trina and I went exploring. We checked out the whole array of cement pool slabs. Around the outside there were partial structures with some stairs. Trina and I walked around all of them. We even came upon a tunnel that was barred up. As I stood in front of it, I felt very powerful energy. I said, "Trina, something wonderful happened in there." She said, "I don't doubt it, but we have to go; the group is leaving." We scooted over and barely caught up with everyone.

We spent a day in Bethlehem. We went to what is thought to be Jesus's birth place.

A church is built on the site now. When we went down into the cave, we were told that this is where Mary gave birth, and this is where she swaddled Jesus. Personally, I didn't feel anything energetically there. I questioned if Jesus was really born there. Possibly He was not even born in Bethlehem. The beautiful thing is that it doesn't really matter.

We were taken to a family-run olive wood workshop and store. We toured the workshop that was in the basement. Only the branches are cut off from the olive trees. They never cut the trees down. We saw a huge pile of olive branches in the basement. We saw the manual machines and tools used to make wooden souvenirs. It was fascinating. There are only three family-run olive wood shops in Bethlehem. Any olive wood items on sale for purchase in Jerusalem are all made in Bethlehem.

While in Jerusalem we walked through dark illumined tunnels in the old city of David.

What a magnificent experience it was to walk through these very ancient ruins. Trina and I held out an arm and hand to brush along the wall as we walked along. Naturally occurring water keeps the walls fairly soft in most places.

As we touched the walls, Trina and I could feel the energy within them.

Paul had planned a healing service at what is called the "Garden Tomb." First we had the opportunity to go inside the tomb. Some say this is where Jesus was laid to rest. When I walked into the tomb, I was surprised that I didn't feel anything energetically.

Paul offered a very moving communion service in an outdoor chapel at the garden. Again I was moved to tears, with feelings of amazing gratitude.

I mentioned to our tour guide, Gershon, that I didn't sense anything in the Garden Tomb. He said that it was not the archaeologically-proven site where Jesus had been laid. He said people love the area there, so they built gardens around a tomb that was there. I shared with him that in the Church of the Holy Sepulcher, which resides in the old city of Jerusalem, I had a profound experience in the lower level. Down there was a small room with a little table and some glass votives with candles. A small group of people were having a ceremony around the table. All around the room was stone. There was a black hole that was covered with black bars. As I stood in front that area, I felt the most intense energy and I was moved to tears. At the end of the day I asked Gershon what the significance of that room was. He smiled at me and said, "That is where archeologists feel the tomb of Jesus was." I was overwhelmed with emotion and gratitude for this incredible blessing I had received.

The last site I will describe is the place where I had the most intense experience and phenomenon of the trip. As our bus headed to this site, I was looking out of the bus window, feeling a bit quiet. I wasn't paying attention when Gershon announced where we were going. I didn't even ask anyone when we left the bus and walked up to a home. As we walked inside the home, I felt an amazing amount of energy right away. The group began to move ahead faster than I. I stayed in the first room, looking in the open spaces. I began to feel as though I were searching for something or someone. My conscious mind did not feel fully present. I wasn't questioning myself or what I was doing. My walking and movements were very slow. I remember seeing Rick behind me. He had assured Paul that he would hold up the line, so that no one was left behind.

I began to leave that first room, still moving ever so slowly. I walked toward a cement spiral staircase. I could hear our group already down below. I remember holding onto the wall. I began crying and hyperventilating. Our group came back up alongside of me and went back up the stairs. I don't know if anyone spoke to me or not. I could feel Rick's presence behind me but heard not a word. At this point, Rick and I were the only two there. I began my way down the stairs quietly saying, "Yeshua." My legs felt like lead. I kept my hands on the wall as I walked, not wanting to be facing straight down. As I reached closer to the bottom, I began sobbing. I finally reached the bottom of the stairs and walked just a foot closer. My eyes looked straight ahead, seeing an overhanging alcove of stone. I could barely allow myself to look at it. It was difficult for me, but I reached down and picked up just three small stones. I made my way slowly up the stairs. Rick was still behind me. I walked outside, with my arms stretched out on the exterior stone wall of house. I began crying and quietly calling out, "Yeshua, Yeshua, Yeshua." No one seemed to be around. Our tour guide, Gershon, looked concerned and asked if I wanted some water. I shook my head no. It was a few minutes before I felt back in my body.

Trina came over and asked if I was okay. "I think so," I said. It was then that I asked her, "Whose house was that anyway?" She told me it was Kaifis's home. She also told me that Jesus was jailed down at the bottom of the stairs around the corner. She said that Kaifis was the High Priest who had put Jesus in jail.

I wasn't sure if I would share this experience in this book, but I decided the story needed to be told. Paul asked me that evening if I would be willing to share what I went through with the group. I did so. I also told them that I felt as if I was someone living back in the time of Jesus who followed his messages. I went on to say that I knew Jesus had been taken and I was looking for him. I'm sure that many of us who are alive today and living spiritual lives were also living at the time of Jesus. I believe that I was finding past life resolution. I feel I experienced this because I was very open to it. I knew from my preparation with meditation and prayers that on this most sacred journey to Israel, I would be shaken to the core of my being.

Through this year, 2014, I have continued offering my healing services at Unity of Greater

Hartford and other venues. I established two new kindred friendships with the Senior Minister of Unity of Greater Hartford, Reverend Mindy Tucker, and her partner, Nickie Golden. I am grateful for their presence of wisdom and joy, which they share greatly with the community.

In July 2014 I felt called to the seclusion of my mountain home in Vermont. I reflected on how I had lived my life to this point. As I laid out my life on paper while feeling at one with nature, it took just seven days to write this book. This time served me greatly. Reflecting upon my life helped me see that every experience serves its purpose.

My life has been a great journey to Living in Grace.

I pray that as you, the reader, absorb my words and my life, you may be touched, renewed, restored, and re-invigorated by the all-encompassing Presence of our Supreme Intelligence, Source of all life and light, Sustainer of all universes. "I am that I am" is my completeness.

Epilogue

In quoting the words of Mahatma Gandhi, "My life is my message," living my joy while moving through life's lessons is a great achievement. As we all know, we have many experiences that can pose challenges. I have received victory with Spirit's unwavering guidance. Victory comes from a deep, intimate relationship with our Creator/Source. I know this Presence. It is my constant, my all, and everything. It is pristine peace that passes all understanding. I have given myself and my life to Presence for the greatest service and purpose of humanity. It is my hope you will do the same.

About the Author

Shari Shea is a devoted healer, light worker, and teacher of truth principles, traveling to many sacred places throughout the United States, as well as Abadiânia, Brazil; Medjugorje; and Israel to deepen her spiritual practices. She has had the honor and privilege to study with renowned mystics Ron Roth and John of God.

Shari offers private lifestyle coaching and energy healing sessions, reminding all brothers and sisters that "All things are possible when we look to the Light within."

As well as coaching and healing, she facilitates meditation and healing services at Unity churches and various venues throughout the Northeast U.S. and New York City.

Shari walks her walk and talks her talk, expressing her favorite quote by Mahatma Gandhi: "My life is my message." She is an avid organic vegetable gardener and spends much time outdoors daily. Her love for nature is a reflection of her spirit.

Shari lives in northern Connecticut with her husband.

For information on Shari Shea's healing work, visit ShariShea.weebly.com.

Printed in the United States
By Bookmasters